TABLE OF CONTENTS

Money Markets & Bonds

How to Safely Earn Higher Rates of Return on Your Savings

D1056071

MOODY PRESS
CHICAGO

ISBN 0-8024-3992-6

Library of Congress Cataloging in Publication Data

1 3 5 7 9 10 8 6 4 2

Printed in the United States of America

FOREWORD

I have known Austin Pryor for almost twenty years now, and I regard him as a good friend. As I have observed him over the years, I have found his counsel to be both biblical and practical. I know of no other individual with whom I would consult with more confidence on the subject of mutual fund investing than Austin.

I believe the true character of an investment adviser is not only the degree of success he has achieved, but the integrity that is maintained in the process. Austin has achieved success in the business world, but, more important, he has done so with truth and honesty.

Obviously you, the reader, must evaluate his advice yourself. No one individual has the right advice for everyone, and anyone can, and will, be wrong in the changing economy we live in. But if you will spend the time to read carefully the counsel Austin provides, you will find it both time and money well spent.

I encouraged my good friends at Moody Press to contact Austin about publishing his writing because I felt he had information that would benefit God's people. We are in no way competitors. Austin and I are collaborators in God's plan to help His people become better stewards of His resources.

Larry Burkett

The biblical principles reflected in this booklet are the foundation for the advice given in *Sound Mind Investing*, my book published by Moody Press. The material in this booklet has, for the most part, been excerpted from that book. As Christians, we acknowledge God as the owner of all. We serve as His stewards with management privileges and responsibilities. The practical application of biblical principles leads us to encourage a debt-free lifestyle and conservative approach to investing such as that shown in what we call the Four Levels of Investing:

Level One: Getting Debt-Free
"The rich rules over the poor, and the borrower becomes the lender's slave."
Proverbs 22:7

Paying off debts which are carrying 12%-18% per year interest charges is the best "investment" move you can make. So, get to work on paying off those credit cards, car loans, student loans, and other short-term debts. Accelerating the payments on your house mortgage, if any, should also be your goal—albeit a longer-term one. It should be your first priority to see the day when you're meeting all current living expenses, supporting the Lord's causes, and completely free of consumer debt.

Level Two: Saving for Future Needs
"There is precious treasure and oil in the dwelling of the wise, but a foolish man swallows it up." Proverbs 21:20

Even if you've not completely reached your Level One goal, it's still a good idea to set aside some money for emergencies or large purchases. A prudent rule of thumb is that your contingency fund should be equal to three to six months' living expenses. We suggest $10,000 as an amount suitable for most family situations.

Level Three: Investing in Stocks
*"Well done, good and faithful servant. You were faithful with a few things,
I will put you in charge of many things." Matthew 25:21*

Only money you have saved over and above the funds set aside in
Level Two should be considered for investing in the stock market.
In Levels One and Two, any monthly surplus was used in a manner
that *guaranteed* you would advance financially—there are no guar-
antees in the stock market. You should initiate a program of stock
mutual fund investing geared to your personal risk temperament
and the amount of dollars you have available to invest.

Level Four: Diversifying for Safety
*"Divide your portion to seven, or even to eight, for you do not know what
misfortune may occur on the earth." Ecclesiastes 11:2*

Once you accumulate $25,000 in your investment account, it's time
for further diversification. By adding investments to your holdings
that "march to different drummers," you can create a more efficient,
less volatile portfolio. The single most important diversification
decision is deciding how much to invest in stocks versus bonds.
That's why determining your personal investing temperament, and
following the guidelines given, can be so helpful.

Free Upon Request

Articles that guide you through the Four Levels—help on getting
debt-free, saving strategies, and updates on specific no-load mutual
fund recommendations that are geared to your personal risk toler-
ance—appear in my monthly newsletter, also called *Sound Mind
Investing*. In it, I offer a conservative investing strategy based on the
careful use of no-load mutual funds. For a free sample copy, simply
return the postage-paid card included at the back of this booklet.

Investing By Lending

I. **Investing is simple because you have only two basic choices.**

    A. There are investments where you become a lender. These are generally the lower-risk kind. The primary risk to watch out for is that you might not get your money back, so the financial strength of the borrower is of great importance.

    B. There are investments where you become an owner. These are generally the higher-risk kind. The primary risk here is that the value of what you own could fall, so the economic outlook and its effect on your holdings is of great importance.

    C. Helping you learn how to safely invest-by-lending is the subject of this booklet.

II. **It's very important that you understand the difference between "yield" and "total return."**

    A. The yield is the amount you receive back on your investment over the course of a year, but expressed in percentage terms rather than dollar terms. This is what we commonly think of as "interest."

B. The total return includes the yield, but also takes into account how much the value of your investment went up or down while you owned it. With investments that fluctuate in value, you won't know your total return *for sure* until you convert your investment back into dollars.

III. The primary advantage of lending your money is the relative safety it offers. There are only two major risks, both of which can be neutralized.

A. The first risk that is you might lend to someone who is not creditworthy. This risk is neutralized by loaning only to the federal government and financially strong companies.

B. The second risk is that you could get locked into a below-market rate of return. This risk is neutralized by loaning only for the very short term.

Investing is simply giving up something now in order to have more of something later.

When you put your money into a savings account, you are making an investment decision (less spendable money now in order to have more spendable money later). When you volunteer your professional services or personal talents now in order to serve in a ministry, you're making an investment decision (less free time or current income now in order to have a greater sense of fulfillment later). When you take a day off without pay in order to spend time with your family, you're making an investment decision (less income now in order to have stronger family ties and happy memories later).

Your desire is simple: Make as much as you can but don't lose any of your savings. You're eager for good advice but wonder who you can trust. You would like to feel confident but usually feel a little confused. You are caught in the constant tension between risk and reward. If you feel this way, I've got good news!

Investing is actually quite simple because you really only have two basic choices: investments where you become *a lender to someone* and investments where you become *an owner of something*.

Investments where you *loan* your money are generally the lower-risk kind. The primary risk is that you might not get your money back, so the financial strength of the borrower is of great importance.

Investments where you *own* something are generally the higher-risk kind. The primary risk here is that the value of what you own could fall, so the economic outlook and its effect on your holdings is of great importance.

The way in which you divide your investment capital between these two basic choices of "loaning" or "owning" has a greater impact on your eventual investment returns *than any other single factor*.

The economic forces that influence the two basic choices are different. It's possible for you to loan your money to a corporation in return for one of its bonds, and have that corporation be financially strong enough to meet all of its interest and principal obligations, even in the midst of a deep recession. On the other hand, it's also probable that if you had invested your money in the stock of the same corporation and become one of its part owners, the same recession would have caused serious harm (hopefully temporary) to the company's earnings and dividend payments. As a part owner of the business, rather than one of its creditors, you would have likely watched the value of your investment in the company lose value.

Of course, that's just looking at the risk part of the equation. The other side of that coin is that the owners of a company can enjoy great prosperity during those times in the business cycle that the economy is healthy and growing. The creditors merely continue receiving the interest payments to which they are due.

All investing eventually finds its way into the American economy. It provides the essential money needed for businesses to be formed and to grow—for engineering, manufacturing, construction, and a million and one other services to be offered and jobs to be created. You can either be a part owner in all this, tying yourself to the fortunes of American business and sharing in the certain risks and possible rewards that being an owner involves. Or, you can play the role of lender, giving your money to others in order to let *them* take the risks and knowing you are settling for a lesser, but more secure, return on your money. Helping you learn how to safely invest-by-lending is the subject of this booklet.

America's largest banks and corporations (not to mention our local, state, and federal governments) need your help...

...they'd like to borrow some money from you. For a few days, months, or, if you're willing, for as long as thirty years. To make sure you get the message, their ads are everywhere. The government promotes safety of principal and has created certain kinds of bonds with special tax advantages. Banks and S&Ls want your deposits and want you to know your money is safe with them because it's "insured." Money market funds, not to be outdone, offer you even better returns and many convenient services. Bond funds tantalize you with suggestions of still higher yields, although in their small print they remind you that "the value of your shares will fluctuate." And of course, insurance companies promote the tax-deferred advantages of their annuities. You're in the driver's seat. To all these institutions, you're a Very Important Person.

Have you ever thought of renting out your money for a while? Chances are, you do it all the time. You probably think of it as a savings account (or certificate of deposit, treasury bill, bond, or fixed annuity), but actually, you're making a loan. The "rent" you're being paid is called interest. In the financial markets, investors with extra money (lenders) loan it out to others who are in need of money (borrowers). One way or another, this market for money involves just about all of us.

First, let's make sure you understand the lingo. You should understand what "yield" means...

...and how it's different from "gain" and "total return." These terms may sound like they're saying the same thing, but they're not, and it's important that you understand the differences.

When evaluating whether an investment has been successful, there are two questions to be addressed. First, how much income from your investment did you receive while you were waiting to get it back? And second, did you get back more than you put in, less than you put in, or the same as you put in?

The income you received while your money was tied up is called the *yield* and is always expressed in annualized terms. If you invest $1,000 in a bond and it pays you $60 every year in *interest*, it is yielding you 6% per year ($1,000/ $60). Now, when you eventually sell your bond, if you receive back more than you paid for it, you have a *capital gain*. Let's say your $1,000 investment is sold after three years for $1,400, giving you a $400 gain. (We'll look at selling at a loss in a second.)

Both the yield and the gain represent partial returns; only when you combine them do you get the total picture, hence the name *total return*. The total return is usually expressed in annual compounded terms. In our example, you invested $1,000 and received back a total of $1,580 over three years ($180 in dividends plus the $400 gain).

By using a financial calculator that can perform time-value-of-money computations, you can learn that it takes a 16.5% per year rate of growth to turn $1,000 into $1,580 in three years. In other words, if you could invest $1,000 at 16.5% for three years, you'd have $1,580 at the end of that time. In the example, you know that part of the growth came from that 6.0% annual yield. But how did you get from 6.0% to that 16.5% total return? By selling for a gain and picking up that extra $400. The 6% *yield* that you received as you went along, *plus* the $400 *gain* at the end, made it possible for you to achieve a very nice 16.5% annualized *total return*.

But what if you had sold at a loss? Say the bond went *down* $400 instead of up $400. That makes the result look quite different. Now you have invested $1,000, and after three years have just $780 ($180 in dividends minus a $400 loss) to show for your efforts. *Your total return is now negative*; while you were collecting your 6% yield with the thought that you were making money, you were actually losing, on average, almost 8% per year!

The yield only tells you part of the story. Your total return is what you're really interested in...

...and you can't know that for certain unless you know exactly how much you'll be getting back and exactly when you'll be getting it. Now here's why all this should be understood by savers. Lending-type investments are often called "fixed income" investments. This refers to the steady flow of interest being paid to the lender, not the market value of the investment. Some fixed income investments—such as insured savings accounts, CDs, and money market funds—do not fluctuate in value. You'll *always* be repaid what you put in, plus any interest you earned; there is never a loss of your original capital to worry about. *That means your total return is always a positive number.*

A TALE OF TWO SAVERS IN 1990

THE ADS PROMISE:

"Our One Year CDs Now Yielding 6%!"

THE ACTUAL RESULT:

Invest on Jan 1:	$1,000
Value of CD on Dec 31:	$1,000
Gain/Loss	-0-
Interest for 1 year at 6%:	+$60
Total Return	$60

THE ADS PROMISE:

"Our Bond Funds Now Yielding 12%!"

THE ACTUAL RESULT:

Invest on Jan 1:	$1,000
Value of fund on Dec 31:	$890
Gain/Loss	-$110
Interest for 1 year at 12%:	+$120
Total Return	$10

MORAL: IT'S THE TOTAL RETURN, NOT YIELD, THAT COUNTS!

There are other fixed income investments, however, that do fluctuate in value day to day. When you eventually sell, you might get back more than you put in or you might get back less. If you get less back, it could even be that you lose more on the sale than you received in interest during the time you owned it. And that means a negative total return!

Look at what happened in the late 1980s. As interest rates fell, the interest paid by CDs and money market funds dropped below what savers had grown accustomed to. In search of higher returns, they saw that some highly-publicized bond funds were "yielding" 12% and more. They thought, *Hey, that looks pretty good!* So off they went. When the junk bond market crashed, investors found they could be receiving a great yield and still lose money! The average high-yield bond fund fell more than 11% in value in 1990. Focusing on yield alone carries high risk because the highest yielding funds are the ones with the lower quality ratings or the longest average maturities.

There are two major risks to watch out for in the world of lending. The first is that you might not get all your money back.

The pros call it the "credit risk" because you're depending on the creditworthiness of the borrower. The U.S. government is still the world's most creditworthy borrower despite the damage done by the irresponsible deficit spending of Congress in recent years. Therefore, borrowers who are in competition with the federal government for your money *must* pay you more in order to give you an incentive to lend to them instead of Uncle Sam. That's why U.S. Treasury bills establish the floor for interest rates. Other rates are higher than the T-bill rate depending on how creditworthy the borrower is.

The second major risk is that you could get locked into a below-market rate of return.

The pros call this the "interest rate risk." It's the same dilemma you face when trying to decide how long you should tie up your money in a bank CD, but it has even greater significance when investing in bonds. If you invest in a two-year CD when it turns out that a six-month one would have been better, you're only missing out on better rates for 18 months. Try making that 18 *years*, and you get an idea of how painful it can be when holding long-term bonds during a period of rising interest rates. This risk can be eliminated by investing in money market funds, the subject of our next section. ◆

Using Money Market Funds to Lend for the Very Short Term

I. **A money market fund is a specialized kind of mutual fund.**

   A. It invests only in very short-term IOUs of the government, big corporations, and banks.

   B. Although not covered by the FDIC, money market funds are essentially as safe as insured bank savings accounts.

   C. Money market funds pay slightly higher returns than bank savings accounts, usually 1% a year and more.

II. **There are three different kinds of money market funds.**

   A. The most common lend primarily to businesses and banks, and typically pay the highest returns.

   B. For those who want added peace of mind, there are money market funds that limit their investments to those securities issued by the federal government.

C. For investors in the higher tax brackets, there are money market funds that invest only in tax-free bonds issued by state and local governments. These pay the lowest returns due to the tax-free feature.

III. **Shopping for a money market fund that offers the best returns and services is easy.**

A. The best yields can be found by looking at the weekly money market fund listings in *Barron's*. Telephone numbers can be obtained from ads in financial magazines or by calling 800 information.

B. Money market funds offer a check-writing service that makes them an excellent way to manage your salary and investment income. You'll want to ask how many checks can be written monthly and the smallest check (dollar amount) that can be written.

C. For added discipline in your savings, you can sign up for automatic transfers—weekly, bi-weekly, or monthly—out of your bank account into your money market fund. Ask for details.

What is a money market fund, anyway?

When you open a savings account or buy a CD at your bank (that is, loaning them your money), your bank turns around and lends your money to others at a higher rate than it's paying to you. Obviously, the less it pays you on your savings, the more profit it makes. The problem with this arrangement is that you and your bank are adversaries.

Fortunately, there are other borrowers, the "big time" players, who would like you to loan to them *and will pay you more interest than your bank will*. These organizations include the federal government, big corporations, and even other banks. However, to readily do business with them, you need a go-between. That's where a special type of mutual fund comes in, one which specializes strictly in the short-term lending of money in the financial markets. Hence, its name: money market fund.

Your money market fund is on *your* side; it will try to get you the best rates it can (while still not taking undue risks). You give the fund your money; the fund gives you one of its shares for every $1 you put in. It takes your money and loans it out to the big time players, almost always getting a rate of interest 1% to 1½% higher than your bank will pay you over the same time period. You can sell your shares and have your money back whenever you want it. And, thanks to Securities & Exchange Commission regulations, money market mutual funds are essentially as safe as insured bank accounts.

With these advantages, you wonder why anyone would still use the traditional bank savings-type accounts. Yet the data shows that hundreds of billions of savers' dollars continue to reside in savings accounts. It seems to me that many savers simply don't understand the difference between bank money market *accounts* and money market *funds* sponsored by mutual fund organizations. They think it's all the same kind of thing. But there's a big difference! Investors in a money market mutual fund receive all of the fund's investment income after very small operational expenses are paid. Depositors in a bank money market account, on the other hand, are merely creditors of the bank and are paid as little as the market will bear. Because it comes out of their pockets, banks naturally want to pay as little as they can get away with. That explains why banks and S&Ls will always offer interest rates lower than money market mutual funds (unless they're desperate for cash, in which case you don't want to loan them your money, anyway).

The value of your money market fund shares doesn't fluctuate; they're kept at a constant $1—the same amount you paid for them. As the fund earns interest from its investments, it "pays" you your portion by crediting you with more shares. You earn interest, that is, receive more shares, every single day. The longer you leave your money in, the more shares you'll have. In this way, you are assured of getting all of your money back, *whenever* you want it, plus all the interest you've earned in the meantime.

There are three different kinds of money market funds.

❶ The most common are the ones that loan money to businesses and banks. I'll refer to these as corporate money market funds because they invest primarily in bank certificates of deposit and *commercial paper*. This kind pays the highest yield to investors and is the most popular. ❷ For people who want added safety, there are money market funds that loan money only to the federal government and its agencies. Given the excellent track record of the corporate kind, it's debatable whether the added caution of sticking strictly with Uncle Sam's securities is worth the slight reduction in yield. For the past fifteen years, the value has been more in the peace of mind investors receive rather than in actually providing additional safety. ❸ For people who are in high tax brackets, there are money market funds that invest only in tax-free municipal bonds that are very close to maturity. The income is free from federal income taxes, and if you invest in a single-state tax-free fund for your state of residence, your income is exempt from state income taxes as well.

BIG BUSINESS

FEDERAL GOVERNMENT

STATE/LOCAL GOVERNMENTS

To intelligently shop for a good money market fund, you need to understand the way their yields are listed in the paper.

Since most of the major money market mutual funds offer similar services and portfolio risk, the decision as to which to buy usually rests on where the best returns are to be found. In researching this information in the newspaper, it is common to find two different yields listed for each fund.

The first percentage listed is usually called the "7 Day Average (or Current) Yield." This reflects the annualized equivalent of what the fund earned for its shareholders over the past week. The limitation of this measure is that it ignores the long-term benefits of daily compounding. So, to more accurately reflect the actual results from investing in a money fund over time, another yield is shown. This percentage is listed second and is called the "7 Day Compounded (or Effective) Yield." This is what an investor would actually earn over a one year period at last week's rate.

The rate of interest you earn changes a little bit every day because the funds have such short average portfolio maturities. This simply means that their "loans" are ultra short-term—almost every day, at least one of these loans is repaid to the fund. The fund must then take this money and loan it out all over again at a new rate. This constant process of re-loaning the money in the pool causes money market fund yields to change rather quickly; last week's rate is somewhat obsolete by the time the data is published. Still, it's helpful for comparison purposes.

The general rule is that you want a long average maturity when rates are falling (so the fund can enjoy the old, higher rates for as long as possible), and you want a short average maturity when rates are rising (so the fund can get its money back quickly and reinvest it in the newer, higher-paying securities).

There is a fiercely waged competition for money market fund deposits (like yours). And one of the principal weapons...

...is a marketing tactic called an "expense waiver." It works like this. Every mutual fund charges "operating expenses" that go to pay the administrative costs of running the fund. Naturally, the lower the expenses, the more income ends up in the pockets of its shareholders. Now, what if a money fund was willing to give up the expenses it was entitled to? Then, all of the gross yield would pass right through to their shareholders. This would put that fund at the top of the yield rankings and would enable it to attract new investors rapidly.

Dreyfus used this tactic in launching its Worldwide Dollar fund. They initially absorbed all of their operating expenses. The resultant higher yields to shareholders enabled Worldwide to quickly become one of the largest money market funds in the country. They have since changed their policy and have

MONEY MARKET MUTUAL FUNDS

A listing of hundreds of taxable and tax-free money market funds appears in most newspapers at least once a week. You can also find one in Barron's and the Thursday edition of The Wall Street Journal.

The Average Maturity indicates the number of days before the average CD or corporate commercial paper is due to be repaid to the fund. The money will then be re-loaned at the current rate. The lower the average maturity, the more quickly the fund will reflect changes in interest rates.

The Effective 7 Day Yield is the number you're interested in. Remember though, when interest rates start moving, these yields will change quickly to reflect the new realities.

Most mutual fund organizations offer at least two kinds of money funds, and some offer three or four.

Most money funds invest primarily in bank CDs and corporate IOUs. They are identified by names like MM, Cash, or Prime.

Fund	Avg Mat	7Day Yld	e7Day Yld	Assets
VanEckUSGovt	48	4.04	4.12	39
VanKampenMM	20	3.26	3.31	28
VangAdmiral US	41	4.00	4.08	1076
VangMMR Fed	41	4.00	4.08	2052
VangMMR Prime	42	4.09	4.17	13361
VangMMR US	41	3.83	3.90	1983
VisionMM	34	4.05	4.13	275
VisionTreas	41	3.81	3.88	225
Vista Federal Prem	60	4.10	4.18	4
Vista Global Prem	73	4.07	4.15	493
Vista Prime Prem	27	4.05	4.13	135
Vista USGovt Prem	27	3.80	3.87	530
Voyager	34	3.40	3.46	35
Vulcan Treasury	39	3.75	3.82	261
WPG Govt MMF	23	3.47	3.53	192
WarburgPincus	47	3.87	3.94	277

The money funds that limit their investments to the U.S. government use names like Treasury, Federal, or simply Govt.

This fund has $493 million in size. Economies of scale can benefit investors once a fund surpasses about $5 billion. Note the Vanguard Prime fund has over $13 billion!

phased it out. That Dreyfus fund has lost its competitive edge, but is counting on its investors to not bother moving their accounts elsewhere just to pick up an extra few tenths of 1% per year. Based on the previous observation that hundreds of billions of dollars are receiving lower returns in bank savings-style accounts because investors are either uninformed or just don't care, I'd have to say that Dreyfus is on pretty safe ground.

Money market mutual funds offer check-writing privileges that make them a much better deal than a similar account at your local bank.

One of the most popular accounts offered by banks and S&Ls is the NOW account, which is basically an interest-bearing checking account. They typically require minimum balances of $1,500 and pay interest of only about 1% less than the leading money funds. Many savers are not aware that a money market mutual fund set up with check-writing privileges is a better alternative. While most money funds request that checks not be written for small amounts (say less than $250), they place no limit on the number of checks written, nor do they charge for the service.

This presents individual savers with the opportunity to safely and quickly improve their rate of return by a full 1% and more. And for businesses, which by law are not permitted to earn interest on their checking account balances, money market mutual funds represent the difference between earning interest or not earning interest. That doesn't seem too difficult a choice.

Here's how to use your money fund as a checking account. First, order a full supply of checks. Usually you'll get no more than a handful unless you make a specific request. Also, you'll want to give written authorization to your fund to make *wire transfers* to your bank (and possibly your brokerage firm) in response to your telephone request.

Second, use your local bank checking account for all salary and investment income deposits. Once a week, transfer the

SHOPPING FOR MONEY MARKET FUNDS

Money and Kiplinger's financial magazines list some of the top yielding money market funds each month. Here are some money market funds from the leading no-load organizations that have had attractive yields in the past. Also, if you have $10,000 or more to invest, many organizations (e.g. Dreyfus, Fidelity, Vanguard) offer money market funds with higher minimums that generally offer better yields—ask about them.

Fund Name	Minimum	Telephone
Benham Prime	$1,000	800-321-8321
Dreyfus 100% U.S. Treasury	2,500	800-782-6620
Evergreen Money Market	2,000	800-235-0064
Fidelity Cash Reserves	2,500	800-544-8888
Strong Money Market	1,000	800-368-3863
USAA Money Market	1,000	800-531-8181
Vanguard Prime Portfolio	3,000	800-662-7447

bulk of your account balance to your money fund. In order to get it to your money market fund even faster, you can ask your bank to "wire it" through the Federal Reserve. Banks charge extra for this service, so you would only want to transfer money this way if the interest you would earn by getting it there a few days faster would exceed the bank wire charge.

Third, pay all bills of $250 and up with a money fund check. This can include your rent or mortgage payments, credit card and auto loan payments, major repairs, insurance, and schooling among others. And last, be sure to let your fund know that you want your canceled checks back. Some funds hold them in their files unless you request them, and this complicates reconciling your monthly statement.

With this arrangement, not only do you earn a market rate of interest on your idle checking balances, but interest is earned until the checks you write clear your money fund (which can take a week or more). Interest earned on routine checking account balances can be significant for an individual and dramatic for a business.

Automation beats procrastination.

Face it. When it comes to saving, it's easy to put it off. So it often helps to have some of your money put aside automatically before you have the opportunity to spend it—set up automatic transfers from your bank account to a money market mutual fund. Such funds typically accept transfers of $50

YEARS REQUIRED TO ACCUMULATE $10,000

IF YOU START WITH	ASSUMING YOU ADD THIS MUCH EVERY WEEK								
	$10	$15	$20	$25	$30	$35	$40	$45	$50
$0	12.2	9.2	7.4	6.2	5.3	4.7	4.2	3.8	3.4
$1,000	10.4	7.9	6.4	5.4	4.7	4.1	3.7	3.3	3.0
$2,000	8.8	6.8	5.6	4.7	4.1	3.6	3.2	2.9	2.7
$3,000	7.3	5.8	4.7	4.0	3.5	3.1	2.8	2.5	2.3
$4,000	6.0	4.8	4.0	3.4	2.9	2.6	2.3	2.1	1.9
$5,000	4.8	3.9	3.2	2.8	2.4	2.1	1.9	1.8	1.6
$6,000	3.7	3.0	2.5	2.2	1.9	1.7	1.5	1.4	1.3

This table assumes that your savings will earn interest at 7% per year. Naturally, there will be occasional periods where this rate is not obtainable. We may be entering such a period now. However, the average money market return over the past decade has been greater than 7%.

and up on either a weekly, every other week, or monthly basis. Most money market mutual funds offer this service; call them and ask for the forms to get started.

Consider a strategy of saving 5%-10% of your gross income when you're in your twenties and moving up to 10%-15% in your thirties and forties. In your fifties, as home buying and child-rearing costs are tapering off, you might be able to boost your savings rate to the 15%-20% area in final preparation for your approaching retirement years. ♦

The Basics of Bonds

I. Bonds are merely long-term IOUs.

    A. They are a promise to repay the amount borrowed at a specific time in the future.

    B. They pay a fixed rate of interest that doesn't vary over the life of the bond.

II. Bond funds have average weighted maturities that are measured in years (versus money market fund maturities of 50-60 days).

    A. The advantage of longer maturities is that you receive a higher yield.

    B. The disadvantages of longer maturities are that the value of your bonds can go down due to either their quality rating being lowered or rising interest rates.

III. Two special kinds of bonds have received much publicity but are usually not suitable for average investors.

    A. Junk bonds are lower-quality bonds that pay higher yields. They are more susceptible to default.

B. Zero coupon bonds make no interest payments to investors. Instead, the interest is allowed to accumulate and is added to the market value of the bond.

Bonds are basically IOUs.

They are a promise to repay the amount borrowed at a specified time in the future. The date at which time the bonds will be paid off is called the *maturity date* and may be set at a few years out or as many as forty years away. At that time, you get back the full face value of the bonds (called *par value*). In order to make bonds affordable to a larger investing public, they are usually issued in $1,000 denominations.

Bonds also promise to pay a fixed rate of interest (called the *coupon rate*) until they are paid off. This rate doesn't vary over the life of the bond. That's why bonds are referred to as "fixed income" investments.

Why buy bonds?

If you want to protect your principal and set up a steady stream of income, then bonds, rather than stocks, are the answer. Current income is traditionally the most important reason people invest in bonds, which usually generate greater current returns than CDs, money market funds, or stocks.

They also can offer greater security than most common stocks since an issuer of a bond will do everything possible to meet its bond obligations.

The interest owed on a corporate bond must be paid to bond holders before any dividends can be paid to the stockholders of the company. And it's payable before federal, state, and city taxes. Being first in line helps make the investment safer. Bond funds diversify among a great many individual bond issues, each of which has its own maturity date. By adding up the length of time until each issue matures and then dividing by the total number of bonds owned, you learn the average amount of time needed for the entire portfolio to mature, that is, to be paid off.

While time is passing, many things can happen to interest rates or to the bond issuer (whoever borrowed the money from investors in the first place) to affect the value of the bonds. The more distant the maturity date, the more time for things to potentially go wrong. That's why bond funds with longer maturities carry more risk than ones with shorter maturities. Any drop in the market value of the bonds is offset against the fund's interest income. If these losses are greater than the interest received by the fund, the price of the bond fund drops that day. *That's why it's possible for investors in a bond fund to get back less than they put in!*

The average maturity of money market portfolios is measured in days; bond funds have portfolios measured in years. The share prices of money market fund shares are set at a constant $1.00 per share; the value of bond fund shares will fluctuate somewhat from day to day. In a money market fund, each day's interest is credited to your account by giving you more shares rather than by increasing the share price; bond funds pay dividends monthly or quarterly. You will always get more back from your money market fund than you put in; it's possible to get less back from a bond fund than you originally invested.

Let's learn by working through an example. XYZ Inc. wants to borrow $200 million for advanced research...

...and doesn't want to have to pay the loan back for 30 years. Rather than ask its banks, which generally don't like to loan their money out for such long periods of time, the company decides to issue some bonds.

Let's say that XYZ agrees to pay a coupon rate of 9% annual interest. Bond traders would call these bonds the "XYZ nines of 2024." (XYZ will pay 9% interest and repay the loan in 2024.) No matter what happens to interest rates over the next 30 years, XYZ is obligated to pay investors 9% per year on these bonds. No more. No less.

Let's say that you decide to purchase one of the XYZ bonds. This means that you will receive $90 per year from XYZ on your $1,000 investment (9% times $1,000). Since bond interest is usually paid twice a year, you would receive two checks for $45 six months apart.

The simplest transaction would work this way. Assume that when XYZ first sells its bonds (through selected stock brokerage firms), you buy one of these brand new bonds at par value. In effect, you loan XYZ $1,000. You collect $90 interest every year for 30 years. It doesn't matter how high or how low interest rates might move during this period, you're still going to get $90 a year because that was "the deal" that you and XYZ agreed to. Finally, in 2024, XYZ pays you back your $1,000. You made no gain on the value of the bond itself; your profit came solely from the steady stream of fixed income you received over the 30 years.

There are two major threats to their financial well-being that all bond investors face. The first is...

...the risk that the bonds will go into default. This means the company that issued them is not able to keep up its interest payments or even to pay off the bonds when they mature. This is the worst-case scenario that faces all bond investors.

To help evaluate this risk, ratings are available that help determine how safe the bonds are as an investment. Standard & Poor's and Moody's are the two companies best known for this. There are nine possible ratings a bond can receive (see page 34). Most bond investors limit their selections to bonds given one of the top four ratings. As you might expect, the lower the quality, the higher rate of interest investors demand to reward them for accepting the increased risk of default.

If XYZ gets into trouble due to poor management and earnings, its ability to pay off its bond debts...

...may come into question. Assume its quality rating is lowered from AAA to A, and that shortly thereafter you need to

WHAT BOND RATINGS MEAN

Standard & Poor's and Moody's are the two leading credit rating agencies. They use slightly different rating codes (S&P on the left, Moody on the right) that attempt to alert bondholders to the relative risks of not being paid the interest when due or the principal upon maturity. The lower the rating, the higher the risk and the higher the interest rate the borrower will have to pay to attract investors.

AAA / Aaa: Highest rating; extremely strong capacity to pay interest and repay principal; smallest degree of investment risk.

AA / Aa: High quality; very strong capacity to pay interest and repay principal; safety margins are strong, but not quite as exemplary as the AAA level.

A / A: Upper-medium grade; strong capacity to pay interest and repay principal; good debt-service coverage, although vulnerable to cyclical trends.

BBB / Baa: Medium grade; adequate capacity to pay interest and repay principal; however, no room for error. Any further deterioration and these will no longer be considered investment grade bonds.

BB / Ba: Speculative grade; only moderately secure.

B / B: Low grade; lacking characteristics of a desirable investment.

CCC / Caa: Very speculative, with significant risk. May be in danger of default.

CC / Ca: Highly speculative, often in default or otherwise flawed; major risk.

C / C: No interest is being paid, or bond is in default.

sell your XYZ bond to meet an unexpected expense. A buyer of your bond will now want greater profits to reward him for the possibly greater risk of default. As a practical matter, it may seem to be a very minor increase in risk, but the buyer will want compensation nevertheless.

But remember, the interest that XYZ pays on these bonds is fixed at $90 per year and can't be changed. The only way anyone buying your bond can improve his profit potential is *if you will lower the price of your bond*. Then, in addition to the interest received from XYZ, the buyer will also reap a profit when he ultimately collects $1,000 (if all goes well) for a bond he bought from you for only, say, $800.

Thus, as the quality rating of a bond falls, we see sellers must lower their asking prices in order to make the bond attractive to buyers. Always remember that a bond can become completely worthless if the issuer gets into financial difficulty and defaults.

How can you minimize the credit risk? First, I should mention a way to eliminate the credit risk altogether: Stick solely with U.S. Treasuries. U.S. government bonds are widely regarded as the world's most creditworthy investments. The interest rates they carry, however, are lower than those of corporate bonds.

In order to obtain higher yields, investors must increase their risk a notch and buy corporate bonds rated AAA, AA, and A. Such bonds typically pay around 1% per year more interest than Treasuries do. Although these bonds are not guaranteed by the government, the companies issuing them are so strong financially that the likelihood of default is very slight. These bonds can be a good compromise between risk and reward for the average investor.

If you're willing to take on even more risk in your desire for higher yields, your search will eventually take you to the "junk bond" market. Brokers and mutual funds have aggressively sold...

...entire portfolios of junk bonds (but they usually call them "high yield" bond funds because that sounds a lot better than "poor quality" bond funds) on the promise of better returns and little risk. But it hasn't worked out that way. For the five years ending June 30, 1992, junk bond funds earned an annual average total return of only 7.8% per year compared with 9.5% for high-grade corporate bond funds. Because investors often fail to understand the risks involved with junk bond funds, I've included a more detailed discussion of them in the final section where I address special purpose bonds like junk, GNMA mortgage bonds, and tax-free bonds. Be sure to read it carefully to make sure you're armed with all the facts and have realistic expectations concerning these bonds as investments.

The second major threat facing bondholders, and the one that is actually the greater of the two, is that the fear of inflation will lead to rising interest rates.

Just for the moment, assume that you're back in 1980 and inflation is running at 12% per year. Now ask yourself this question: would you be willing to pay full price for a 30-year, $1,000 bond with a 9% coupon rate? Not likely. The bond would only be paying you $90 in interest per year at a time when you need $120 just to keep up with inflation. You'd be agreeing to a deal that would guarantee you a loss of purchasing power of $30 each year. Eventually, you'd get your $1,000 back, but it wouldn't buy nearly as much then as it does now.

But what if the seller would lower the price of the bond so you could buy that bond at a big discount? If you only had to pay $750 for a $1,000 bond, it might make economic sense. The $90 interest per year—remember, the coupon rate stays fixed throughout the life of the bond—would represent a 12% return ($90 received in interest divided by the $750 invested). Now, at least you're even with inflation. Plus, when the bond matures 30 years down the road, you get a full $1,000 back for your $750. That's 33% more than you paid for it.

So you can see that high inflation (or even the fear of high inflation) causes bond buyers to demand a higher return on their money in order to protect their purchasing power. And in order to create that higher return, bond sellers must lower their asking prices. That's why the bond market usually goes down when any news comes out that could reasonably be interpreted as leading to higher consumer prices.

NEW YORK

Surprise! Did you know you can buy bonds on the New York and American Stock Exchanges? These are bonds that were issued in the past and are now being bought and sold in what's called the "secondary" market (the primary market is when new bonds are sold to investors when they

BONDS	CUR YLD		VOL	CLOSE	NET CHG	
AldSig 9 7/8	97	9.2	21	107 3/4	-	3/8
ATT 5 5/8	95	5.7	145	99 1/2	+	1/8
Amoco 7 7/8	96	7.6	15	103 1/8	-	3/4
Banka 8 7/8	05	8.7	55	102 1/4	+	1/4
BellPa 7 1/8	12	7.7	43	92 1/2	+	1/8
BethSt 8.45s	05	9.3	73	90 3/8	+	3/8
Bordn 8 3/8	16	8.4	33	100	- 1	1/2
Chiquta 11 7/8	03	11.3	98	105 3/8	-	1/2

Name	Maturity Date	Volume
is the company that borrowed the money initially and is (1) responsible for paying the interest regularly and (2) paying the amount owed on the bond when it matures.	is the year when the bond matures. Only the last two digits are shown. This Borden bond issue would be known as the "eight and three-eighths of sixteen" and would mature in 2016.	is the dollar value (expressed in thousands) of all the bonds of this issue that traded yesterday. $145,000 of this AT&T bond traded. The bigger, the better, because it means you have lots of buyers and sellers—which is what you want because it will help the market be more efficient and you'll get a better price.

EXCHANGE BONDS

are first issued). The secondary market is where you go to sell a bond you bought when it first came out, but then changed your mind and decided you didn't want to hold it for 20 years after all. Your broker, who is a member of the Exchange, can sell it for you there just like stocks.

BONDS		CUR YLD	VOL	CLOSE	NET CHG	
ChryF 9.30s	94	9.2	175	100 5/8	+	1/8
Chrysir 8s	98	8.4	9	94 7/8	+	3/4
Citicp 8.45s	07	8.6	29	98 1/4	+	1/4
CmwE 7 5/8	03F	7.8	4	98	+	7/8
DetEd 9.15s	00	9.0	6	101 1/2	−	1 1/2
duPnt 8.45s	04	8.3	29	102	+	1/8
Exxon 6s	97	6.2	20	97 1/2	+	3/8
GMA 7.85s	98	7.8	40	101	−	3/4

Coupon Rate

is the interest the borrower pays to the bondholder. It stays constant throughout the life of the bond. Since bonds usually come in $1000 denominations, this DuPont bond pays $84.50 per year interest (8.45% x $1000).

Current Yield

is the number you're interested in as a buyer. It tells what your return would be if you bought the bond at yesterday's closing price of $1020 for a $1000 bond. It's computed by dividing your annual interest by the amount you invest ($84.50 divided by $1020 = 8.28%).

Net Change

is almost always the result of movements in interest rates. As we'll soon see, bond prices and interest rates move in opposite directions. Since most of these changes indicate that bond prices rose, it's reasonable to assume that interest rates fell the previous day. See next page.

Here's how this affects your XYZ bond. Although you originally intended...

...to hold onto your XYZ bond for the full 30 years, real life is rarely quite that simple. Very few investors hold onto their bonds for so long a period of time. Let's say that you decide to sell your XYZ bond and use the money for a really worthwhile purpose—like buying tickets to the Final Four basketball championship. You want your money back *now*, not in 2024.

Where do you sell it? In the bond market where older bonds (as opposed to new ones just being issued) are traded. Your stockbroker can handle it for you. Assuming that XYZ is still in tip-top financial condition with a AAA credit-rating, you expect to get all of your $1,000 back. Well, maybe you will, and maybe you won't. The big question is: What is the rate of interest being paid by companies that are now issuing new bonds?

If the rate of interest being paid on new bonds is higher than what your bond pays, you've got a problem. (Let's assume that interest rates have gone up since you bought your XYZ bond, and that new bonds of comparable quality are now paying 11%.) Why would any investor want to buy your old XYZ bond that will pay him just $90 per year in interest when he can buy a new one that will pay $110? Obviously, if both bonds cost him the same price, he wouldn't. So, to sell your bond you will have to reduce your asking price below $1,000 to be competitive and attract buyers.

On the other hand, if interest rates have *fallen,* to let's say 8%, then the shoe is on the other foot. Your old bond that pays $90 per year looks pretty attractive compared to new ones that pay only $80. This means you can sell it for a premium, meaning more than the $1,000 par value you paid.

Here's the lesson: Any time you sell a bond before its maturity date, it will likely be worth less than you paid for it

BOND PRICES FALL WHEN INTEREST RATES RISE

This graph shows the various effects on short-term, medium-term, and long-term bond portfolios when interest rates go up. The point is not only that interest rates and bond prices move opposite to each other, but also that the longer term the bond, the greater the price movement.

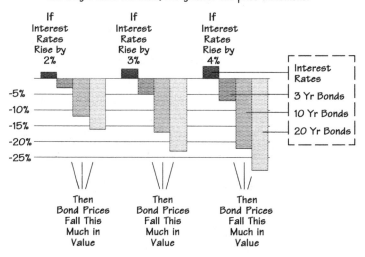

(because interest rates have gone up since you bought it) or worth more than you paid for it (because interest rates have gone down since you bought it).

That's why it's possible to lose money even with investments like U.S. Treasury bonds. They're safe from default, but nobody can protect you against rising interest rates.

Of course, if you hold onto your XYZ bond until it matures in 2024, it will be worth $1,000. At that time, XYZ will repay the par value to whoever owns its bonds. The closer you get to a bond's maturity date, the more the bond's price reflects its full face value. That's why interest rates eventually lose their power to affect the market value of a bond.

The longer you have to wait until maturity, the longer you are vulnerable. How can you shorten the wait (and therefore reduce the risk)? Buy old bonds that were issued many years back and are now only a few years from their maturity. The shorter the maturity, the less volatile a bond's price will be.

Short-term bonds, then, represent a middle ground between the money market and the long-term bond market. They have much less interest rate risk than long-term bonds and still pay higher yields than money market funds.

When it comes to bonds that carry a high interest-rate risk, zero-coupon bonds are the ultimate!

Would you be interested in buying bonds that pay "zero" interest? That's right, no interest at all. Doesn't sound very appealing, does it? But what if I was willing to sell you a three-year $1,000 zero-coupon bond for $700? Invest $700 for three years and get $1,000 back. If you said yes, good move! Although you would be receiving no interest for three years, when you finally got your $1,000 it would represent an effective yield of +12.64% per year before taxes.

"Zeros" are bonds that pay no interest but are sold at deep discounts from their face value. Why is this good? For the average investor, it's not. Zeros have two unpleasant drawbacks. First, even though you're not receiving any interest, the IRS taxes you on the increase in the value of your "zeros" even though you won't actually receive any profits until they mature. Second, zeros are much more sensitive to changes in interest rates. As a result, their market prices rise and fall much more dramatically than regular bonds as rates fluctuate. If all goes well with the issuer, the zero bonds will be worth their full face value when they mature, but if you need to sell them prior to maturity in a climate of rising interest rates, you might be shocked at how much they have dropped in value.

As you can probably tell, I'm not that excited about "zeros." But if you truly desire to buy some, here are my suggestions: (1) wait until you have reason to believe that interest rates are at or near a peak; (2) buy only the U.S. treasury kind; (3) buy only as many as you are fairly certain you can afford to hold until they mature; and (4) buy them only in your IRA or Keogh in order to escape the income taxes. ♦

Shopping for Bond Funds

I. **By using the two main influences on risk, we can create a "risk profile" for categorizing bond funds that will greatly simplify the process of selecting the bond funds that are best for you.**

   A. First, I will divide all bond funds into two groups: those that invest only in bonds of the highest quality (which we'll call the "superior quality" group) and those that are willing to invest in lesser-rated bonds in a search for higher yields (which we'll call the "mixed quality" group).

   B. Second, I'll subdivide each of these two groups further: those funds with medium/short-term maturities in their portfolios (which we define as less than seven years) and those with longer-term maturities (which we define as seven years and longer).

   C. This results in four distinct categories (or "peer groups"), each having its own risk characteristics in terms of quality and average maturities.

II. I'll point out risk characteristics you should understand and suggest four specific no-load funds in each group that have been top performers in their peer group in recent years. You can investigate them further if you have an interest in a particular risk category.

How do you distinguish among the large number of bond mutual funds and select the ones most appropriate for you?

There are many varieties of bond funds. They differ in whether they're committed to investing in high quality bonds or will settle for higher-risk, higher-yielding ones, which, of course, will be of lower quality. They differ in the maturities of their portfolios—some seek to keep their average weighted maturities at three years or less, others want to keep theirs at no less than 20 years. Some generate taxable dividends, others tax-free dividends. Some limit themselves to the U.S. market, whereas others are permitted to invest overseas. Now imagine that you started mixing and matching all these possibilities to see how many different combinations are possible. The answer? A lot! More than you want to read about.

I've grouped bond funds in a way that should be most helpful for beginners.

These aren't the "official" groupings; in fact, there's no such thing. The Investment Company Institute, which is the trade association for the mutual fund industry, has its way of grouping funds. Morningstar and Lipper, the two major mutual fund reporting services, have their own ways—and each is different from the other. As the Big Three can't agree on an official system for classifying bond funds, I have devised a system that should be more user friendly for you.

First, I initially set aside the international bond funds because they have special characteristics requiring careful handling. I put them in their own "special purpose" category. I then take the U.S. funds and divide them into two groups. *One group is my "plain vanilla" group, composed of those funds*

IMPORTANT INFORMATION ABOUT HOW BOND FUNDS ARE CLASSIFIED ACCORDING TO RISK IN THIS BOOKLET

I have created my own way of classifying bond funds that I believe you will find relatively easy to understand and use. You should know, however, that I have applied definitions that are not commonly used within the investment industry. For example, in my ratings of bond quality, I don't make a distinction between a fund invested only in U.S. government-backed bonds versus one that also invests in AAA-rated corporate bonds. Technically, of course, the government bonds are of higher quality, but from a practical point of view the AAA-rated corporate bonds are also quite safe. In terms of risk, the differences are insignificant.

Another example would be the way I set the cutoff for long-term bonds at just 7 years. Most would say a bond should be at least 10 years away from maturity before considering it to be long-term. By using the lower number, I am erring on the side of caution to protect you against bond fund losses during periods of rising interest rates. So keep in mind that what you find presented in this booklet has been simplified to make learning and investing easier for you.

that invest in a diversified portfolio of bonds that are taxable and have no unusual features. These are the funds I regard as primary when assembling a bond portfolio. The other group is a second "special purpose" group of bond funds with special features. This group includes high yield (junk) bonds, mortgage-backed bonds, and tax-exempt bonds. We'll discuss the characteristics of these bonds in section five.

Now it's time to subdivide the primary group into four smaller subgroups. I'll illustrate this for you as we go along by using a graphic device, which I call a "risk profile," and dividing it into four diamond-shaped compartments. As we've discussed, there are two major threats facing lenders. The first is the risk that the bonds will go into default. The wide diversifi-

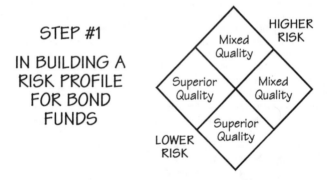

STEP #1

IN BUILDING A RISK PROFILE FOR BOND FUNDS

HIGHER RISK

Mixed Quality

Superior Quality

Mixed Quality

Superior Quality

LOWER RISK

Funds will be assigned to either the "top quality" or "mixed quality" half of the profile depending on the proportion of lower quality-rated corporate bonds in their current portfolios.

cation you can achieve in a bond mutual fund greatly lessens the impact of one or two defaults; still, defaults reduce your overall return. *This risk can be virtually eliminated by investing only in the highest quality portfolios.* As we create our risk profile, step one involves assigning our best quality funds to the lower diamonds (indicating low risk). The funds in this group invest in (1) any kind of government security, typically notes and bonds issued by the U.S. Treasury and various federal agencies; and (2) high quality bonds (rated AAA down to A) of big corporations. As far as safety of principal is concerned, the U.S. government isn't going to default, and it is extremely rare for a high-grade corporate bond to do so.

Bond funds of mixed quality are assigned to the higher diamonds (indicating higher risk). What I'm calling "mixed quality" are usually referred to as "general corporate" bond funds in the financial media. That's misleading because many funds classified this way also invest in Treasury securities as well (in order to balance out some of their risk and also to put idle cash to good use in case they can't find enough of the lesser grade bonds they like). So since they obviously can own large amounts of governments, you shouldn't think of them as just buying bonds issued by businesses. What the name is meant to imply is that these funds can invest in a mix of corporates (of all kinds of quality) *if they want to* in an attempt to increase their yields. By mixing these in, the overall credit quality of their portfolios drops.

The second step in developing our risk profile involves taking a bond portfolio's maturity into consideration.

The second risk of owning bonds is that of rising interest rates—as rates go up, bond prices go down. The sooner the bonds in your portfolio mature, the sooner your bond fund manager can go out and invest at the new higher rates. As you move toward longer maturities, the risk of being hurt by rising interest rates increases. We reflect this in step two as shown below: because the medium-to-short term portfolios pose the least risk, we assign them to the lowest diamond. The long-term portfolios have the highest risk and so occupy the highest of the four diamonds.

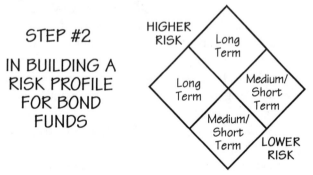

STEP #2

IN BUILDING A
RISK PROFILE
FOR BOND
FUNDS

HIGHER RISK

Long Term

Long Term

Medium/ Short Term

Medium/ Short Term

LOWER RISK

Funds will be assigned to either the "long-term" or "medium/short-term" half of the profile depending on the weighted maturities of their current bond portfolio. Seven years and up is counted as long-term, less than 7 years as medium/short term.

Now for the final step where we put all this together. As you can see in the illustration on page 52, the two fundamental risk considerations combine to create four distinctive risk categories. The category that is lowest in the profile (the diamond designated number 1) is also the category with the lowest risk because it combines the safety of high quality bonds with shorter maturities. The category that is highest in the profile (the diamond designated number 4) is the category with the highest risk because it features bonds of mixed quality that also have long-term maturities. The two diamonds in the center are medium in risk; however, because a shorter-term portfolio—even one of mixed quality—is more stable than a higher quality long-term portfolio, I assigned the lower risk number 2 to that category.

We'll spend the rest of this section taking a closer look at each of these four risk categories. For each one, I have supplied names of some no-load bond funds in that category which you can evaluate further should you wish to invest in that kind of bond fund.

Don't be confused if the *name* of a bond fund appears to contradict the category in which I have placed it. A fund is given a name that reflects its general objectives as spelled out in its prospectus. The name given reflects the *anticipated* investments that a fund's portfolio manager will make; I have placed them according to the *actual* investments in the portfolio in mid-1992.

BUILDING A "RISK DIAMOND" FOR BOND FUNDS: STEP #3

Now we can assign each of 188 bond funds to one of the four risk diamonds depending upon their current portfolio holdings. A fund's risk category can change if its portfolio holdings change sufficiently; the numbers below reflect an analysis done in 1992.

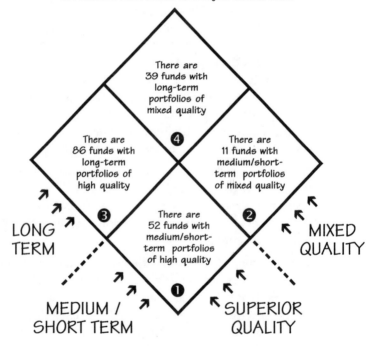

The lowest-risk funds are found in diamond ❶, the next lowest in diamond ❷, and so on.

Naturally, fund holdings are constantly changing, and it is possible for there to be dramatic portfolio changes between the time this booklet is written and the time you read it. Be sure to verify the current data with all the funds you are considering as possible investments. ◆

Characteristics of Medium/Short-Term High Quality Bond Funds

These funds invest in bonds of the U.S. government and its agencies, and large corporations whose bonds are primarily credit-rated AAA, AA, or A. On average, the bonds in these portfolios come due for payment in less than seven years. These are the safest kind of bonds to hold during periods of rising interest rates due to their shorter maturities. Those with maturities of three years or less can also serve as higher yielding substitutes for money market funds if you're willing to accept some minor interest-rate risk.

No-Load Funds in This Category You Might Consider	Scudder Short-Term Bond	Benham Treasury Note	Vanguard F/I Short-Term Corp	Dreyfus 100% US S/T
Morningstar Risk Category	Corp Hi Quality	Gvt Treasury	Corp Hi Quality	Gvt Treasury
Avg Return 1991-93	9.3%	9.3%	9.1%	8.9%
Total Return for 1993	8.2%	7.8%	6.9%	6.9%
Total Return for 1992	5.5%	6.6%	7.3%	7.0%
Total Return for 1991	14.3%	13.7%	13.1%	12.9%
Total Return for 1990	9.9%	9.2%	9.2%	6.2%
Total Return for 1989	13.3%	11.9%	11.3%	12.8%
Minimum Purchase	$1,000	$1,000	$3,000	$2,500
Toll Free: Call 1-800	225-2470	472-3389	662-7447	645-6561
Nasdaq Ticker Symbol	SCSTX	CPTNX	VFSTX	DRTSX

Source: Morningstar Mutual Funds OnDisc © Morningstar, Inc. 53 West Jackson Blvd., Chicago, IL 60604. (800) 876-5005. Although gathered from reliable sources, data accuracy cannot be guaranteed. By the time you read this, these funds may have characteristics different from those shown. These are not recommended funds per se, but are offered as worthy of consideration. Contact the fund for current information before you invest.

Characteristics of Medium/Short-Term Mixed Quality Bond Funds

Many of the same kinds of government and AAA corporate bonds appear in the "mixed quality" funds as are in the high-quality ones. The difference is in what else you'll find—a much higher percentage of BBB corporate bonds and others rated as low as BB and B. If the portfolio manager is good at picking "the best of the bunch" among the thousands of bonds that don't have the financial muscle to get an A or better rating, the payoff is a higher total return than the high-quality group usually offers.

No-Load Funds in This Category You Might Consider	Strong Short-Term Bond	Fidelity Short-Term Bond	Strong Advantage	Dreyfus Short-Term Income
Morningstar Risk Category	Corp General	Corp General	Corp General	Corp General
Avg Return 1991-93	10.2%	9.9%	9.0%	new
Total Return for 1993	9.3%	8.5%	8.1%	9.0%
Total Return for 1992	6.7%	7.4%	8.4%	new
Total Return for 1991	14.6%	14.0%	10.6%	new
Total Return for 1990	5.3%	5.8%	6.6%	new
Total Return for 1989	8.2%	10.5%	9.5%	new
Minimum Purchase	$1,000	$2,500	$1,000	$2,500
Toll Free: Call 1-800	368-1030	544-8888	368-1030	645-6561
Nasdaq Ticker Symbol	SSTBX	FSHBX	STADX	DSTIX

Source: Morningstar Mutual Funds OnDisc © Morningstar, Inc. 53 West Jackson Blvd., Chicago, IL 60604. (800) 876-5005. Although gathered from reliable sources, data accuracy cannot be guaranteed. By the time you read this, these funds may have characteristics different from those shown. These are not recommended funds per se, but are offered as worthy of consideration. Contact the fund for current information before you invest.

Characteristics of Long-Term High Quality Bond Funds

This is the next-to-the-highest risk category. It's not a question of quality—these funds invest in bonds of the U.S. government and its agencies, and large, creditworthy corporations whose bonds are primarily credit-rated AAA, AA, or A. It's the longer maturities, which average 12.5 years for the funds in this group. The longer maturities dramatically increase volatility. These funds are great to buy only if you're willing to lock in the current level of interest rates for years to come.

No-Load Funds in This Category You Might Consider	Dreyfus 100% Long-Term	Vanguard F/I Long-Term US	Scudder Income	Benham L/T Treas &Agency
Morningstar Risk Category	Gvt Treasury	Gvt Treasury	Corp Hi Quality	Gvt General
Avg Return 1991-93	14.0%	13.8%	12.2%	new
Total Return for 1993	16.5%	16.7%	12.7%	17.6%
Total Return for 1992	7.6%	7.4%	6.7%	new
Total Return for 1991	18.3%	17.4%	17.3%	new
Total Return for 1990	7.0%	5.8%	8.3%	new
Total Return for 1989	16.2%	17.9%	12.8%	new
Minimum Purchase	$2,500	$3,000	$1,000	$2,500
Toll Free: Call 1-800	645-6561	662-7447	225-2470	472-3389
Nasdaq Ticker Symbol	DRGBX	VUSTX	SCSBX	DSTIX

Source: Morningstar Mutual Funds OnDisc © Morningstar, Inc. 53 West Jackson Blvd., Chicago, IL 60604. (800) 876-5005. Although gathered from reliable sources, data accuracy cannot be guaranteed. By the time you read this, these funds may have characteristics different from those shown. These are not recommended funds per se, but are offered as worthy of consideration. Contact the fund for current information before you invest.

Characteristics of Long-Term Mixed Quality Bond Funds

With this group, we're at the top of the risk profile. It's not just that these portfolios hold a fair amount of BBB and below rated bonds—the credit risk is reduced by the broad diversification a mutual fund offers. It's those long maturities! On average, the bond funds in this category have portfolio maturities of more than thirteen years. If you buy them at the low end of the interest rate cycle and then rates begin to move up, not only will you have locked in low yields, but the value of your bonds will fall as well.

No-Load Funds in This Category You Might Consider	Fidelity Investment Grade	Strong Income	Harbor Bond	SteinRoe Income
Morningstar Risk Category	Corp General	Corp General	Corp General	Corp General
Avg Return 1991-93	14.2%	13.6%	13.6%	13.1%
Total Return for 1993	15.6%	16.8%	12.4%	13.2%
Total Return for 1992	8.3%	9.4%	9.1%	9.1%
Total Return for 1991	18.9%	14.8%	19.7%	17.2%
Total Return for 1990	6.1%	-6.2%	7.9%	6.1%
Total Return for 1989	13.0%	0.4%	13.7%	7.1%
Minimum Purchase	$2,500	$1,000	$2,000	$1,000
Toll Free: Call 1-800	544-8888	368-1030	422-1050	338-2550
Nasdaq Ticker Symbol	FBNDX	SRNCX	HABDX	SRHBX

Source: Morningstar Mutual Funds OnDisc © Morningstar, Inc. 53 West Jackson Blvd., Chicago, IL 60604. (800) 876-5005. Although gathered from reliable sources, data accuracy cannot be guaranteed. By the time you read this, these funds may have characteristics different from those shown. These are not recommended funds per se, but are offered as worthy of consideration. Contact the fund for current information before you invest.

Special Purpose Bond Funds: Junk, Tax-Frees, and Ginnie Maes

I. Junk bonds are bonds with quality-ratings below BBB. The investment industry prefers to call them "high yield" bonds.

A. These bonds carry higher yields to reward investors for accepting the higher risk that the bond issuer might default.

B. The funds that specialize in junk bonds expect some defaults in their portfolios but believe that their wide diversification will limit the damage. They expect the high yields to help them come out ahead even after allowing for a few defaults.

C. I don't recommend junk bonds for investors unless they understand the risks and the bonds fit a specific purpose within their long-range plan.

II. Tax-free bonds are those issued by state and local governments.

A. The interest received from tax-free bonds is exempt from federal income tax and also exempt from state income tax in the state where the bond is originally issued.

B. Because of the tax benefit, these bonds pay less interest than taxable bonds of comparable quality.

C. City and state governments are under increasing financial strains. This makes it very important for investors to stay with tax-free bonds that have quality ratings of A and better.

III. **Mortgage bonds backed by the Government National Mortgage Association are called Ginnie Maes.**

A. They offer attractive yields and pay monthly dividends.

B. The disadvantage of Ginnie Maes is the "prepayment risk" experienced when homeowners refinance their mortgages at lower rates.

C. As with other medium-term bonds, their yields and market values will fluctuate moderately.

Junk bonds are corporate bonds that have been given low ratings by independent grading firms...

...such as Moody's and Standard & Poor's. The ratings are intended to evaluate a company's financial strength and, accordingly, its ability to pay both the principal and interest on its debts as they come due. Generally, only bonds rated in the top three categories (AAA, AA, and A) are considered "investment grade" quality. Only a few hundred of the strongest companies qualify for these high ratings.

That leaves several thousand companies stuck with the "junk" label, although naturally there are differences in financial strength even here. If you want the higher yields that these companies offer (in order to entice investors to buy their bonds), the trick is to sort through these lower-rated offerings and pick the strongest of the weak. That's the task of the fund manager.

Junk bond investors are realistic enough to expect some of their holdings to eventually default. Studies have shown that it's normal for 1.5% to 2.5% of all junk bonds to default in any given year. That's why the diversification provided by the fund is so essential—it spreads out this risk over a sufficiently large number of bonds to reasonably assure that its default experience will be in this range. The higher yields paid by junk bonds compensate investors for this expected small loss of capital.

Here's how it might work. Say the average yield in the fund portfolio is 12% on junk bond holdings of $1 million. That means the fund would receive $120,000 in interest payments throughout the year. Assume that the fund experiences a 2.5% default rate ($25,000 of their bond holdings). Even in a default, bonds don't typically become worthless; bondholders usually recoup 40%-50% of the principal value of the bonds. If the fund recouped 40% of its investment in the bad bonds, it would get $10,000 of its capital back. That means the fund lost $15,000 on the defaulting bonds, which would be offset against the interest income. After all is said and done, the fund would still come out $105,000 ahead for the year.

A healthy economy is very important to buyers of junk bonds because it helps maintain a positive cash flow that enables even weaker companies to keep up with their interest payments. While a recession spells trouble for everybody, it can be especially devastating for companies with high debt loads. It's the same problem faced by families with high credit card and other consumer debt.

With these risk/reward characteristics in common, it's not surprising to see how the junk bond fund group often marches more with the average stock fund than it does with other bond funds. In 1991, high-quality bond funds were up about 15%, and stock and junk bond funds, even though the economy was in a recession, were up a surprisingly strong

33% and 37%, respectively. Why? Because, like the stock market, junk bonds are valued based on *anticipated events* in the economy six to nine months away. Investors began expecting the recovery to kick in and greatly improve the cash flow of the companies that had issued the bonds. (Junk bonds flourished during the strong economies of 1986 and 1988.) This appeared to lower the risk, and the high yields looked great in comparison to other savings-type investments, which had fallen to extremely low levels. And so the rush was on.

Are junk bonds for you? Not unless you understand (and can afford) the risks and intend to hold them for 3-5 years. Because of the risks, spreading your investments over three or four no-load funds will diversify your risk. And because of their volatility, I suggest using dollar-cost-averaging to minimize the chance that you might be making a major commitment at precisely the wrong time.

Tax-free bonds: they're not for everybody.

Tax-free bonds (also called "municipal" bonds) are debt securities issued by state and local governments. By law, the interest earned on such bonds is exempt from federal taxes. If the issuer is a city in your state, or the state itself, the interest is also exempt from the state income tax. Because of the value of these tax benefits, issuers of tax-free bonds can borrow money at interest rates lower than those paid by other borrowers. That means they won't pay as much in interest, but what tax-free funds do pay, you can keep entirely!

Would you benefit from investing in tax-free bonds? That depends on your "marginal" tax bracket. The federal tax law provides for three basic tax brackets—15%, 28%, and 31%—to be applied against "adjusted gross income." Married couples, filing jointly, currently pay a 15% tax on their first $34,000, a 28% tax on any amount between $34,000 and $82,150, and 31% on any AGI over $82,150. How high up the tax ladder does your income take you? That's your marginal rate.

Here's an easy calculation you can make to see if you're better off receiving a higher rate of interest that is taxable or a lower return that is tax-free...

...First, subtract your marginal rate from "1." Second,

WOULD TAX-FREES GIVE YOU A BETTER RETURN?

That depends on your marginal tax bracket!
Here's how to make the calculation...

For a 15% Marginal Tax Bracket Investor
1 minus .15 = .85
The 4% tax-free rate divided by .85 =
a 4.71% pre-tax rate

For a 28% Marginal Tax Bracket Investor
1 minus .28 = .72
The 4% tax-free rate divided by .72 =
a 5.56% pre-tax rate

For a 31% Marginal Tax Bracket Investor
1 minus .31 = .69
The 4% tax-free rate divided by .69 =
a 5.80% pre-tax rate

divide the yield of the tax-free bond by the resulting number. This formula converts the after-tax yield of the tax-free bond to its *equivalent before-tax yield*. Then you can compare apples with apples. Let's walk through an example. Assume that one-year bank certificates of deposit (CDs) are paying 5½%, and you can buy a high-quality tax-free bond that pays 4%. Which would give you the higher after-tax return? Using the two-step calculation, we can convert the 4% tax-free yield to its equivalent before-tax yield.

These simple calculations show how large a fully taxable yield must be in order to equal that of the tax-free bond: 4.71% for the 15% taxpayer, 5.56% for the 28% taxpayer, and 5.80% for the 31% taxpayer. Since the CD pays a taxable 5.50% yield, it's clearly a better deal for the 15% taxpayer. For the 28% tax-bracket investor, however, there's not much difference. Only for the 31% taxpayer is it clearly more profitable to take the 4% tax-free bond.

There is even more incentive to switch to tax-frees if you live in a high-tax state. There are some so-called "single state" tax-exempt funds...

...that invest solely in tax-free securities issued from within that one state. This means the interest income is *double tax-free*: from state income taxes as well as federal ones. This brings us to another factor that complicates the computation.

New Yorkers, for example, could have combined federal, state, and local taxes totaling as high as 38%. For such a taxpayer, investing in a New York-only tax-free fund yielding 5.6% would generate an equivalent before-tax return of 9.03%. Since this is higher than the conventional money funds' 8.0%, it makes sense from a tax point of view for some investors.

Be aware, however, that a huge amount of diversification protection is lost with this approach. It seems to me this is a significant drawback—you'll have all your muni investments riding

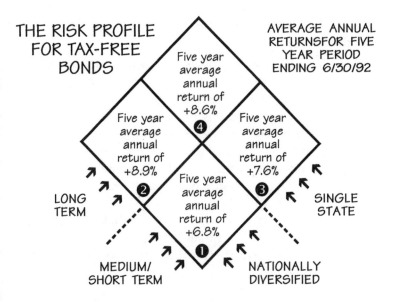

THE RISK PROFILE FOR TAX-FREE BONDS

AVERAGE ANNUAL RETURNS FOR FIVE YEAR PERIOD ENDING 6/30/92

Five year average annual return of +8.6%
❹

Five year average annual return of +8.9%
❷

Five year average annual return of +7.6%
❸

Five year average annual return of +6.8%
❶

LONG TERM

SINGLE STATE

MEDIUM/ SHORT TERM

NATIONALLY DIVERSIFIED

on the financial condition of only your state and its financial strength. For example, the state of Massachusetts' well-publicized financial difficulty in 1990 led to a lowering of its credit rating. Bond buyers would no longer pay the same price for Massachusetts tax-free bonds—they demanded additional discounts and bond values plunged. With concerns mounting about the financial health of several of our major cities and states, many analysts question the wisdom of placing much of one's savings at higher risk merely to save a percent or so on taxes.

When it comes to the safety of tax-free bonds, let the buyer beware!

It is estimated that individuals already own $450 billion of these tax-exempt securities, and, with taxes creeping higher nationwide, the popularity of municipal bonds seems sure to grow. Unfortunately, this growing attraction to munis comes at a time when many states and cities are under increasingly difficult financial pressures. Years of overspending have combined with reduced federal revenue-sharing and regional recessions to drastically weaken the finances of state and local governments. The result is a lowering of the overall quality of the tax-free bond market. Standard & Poor's gives only 34% of today's munis its "high quality" rating of AA or better. One expert estimates that about one-third of the muni market is on its way to becoming the junk bonds of the 1990s. If you believe you would benefit from investing in tax-free bonds, I strongly encourage you to diversify widely to minimize the risk of defaults. This can easily be accomplished by investing in three no-load muni funds rather than putting all your money into just one.

Many funds have purchased insurance policies that insure

TAX-EXEMPT BONDS

Issue	Coupon	Mat.	Price	YTM
Allegheny Co Pa Air 92B	6.625	01-01-22	98¼	6.77
Calif Comm Develop	6.750	12-01-21	99½	6.79
Chesapeake Bay Bridge	6.375	07-01-22	96½	6.65
Fla Bd Ed Pb Ed Cap	6.700	08-01-22	99¾	6.72
Fla Pollution Ref Rev	6.625	01-01-27	97¾	6.79
Harris Co Toll Rd Tex92	6.500	08-15-11	98	6.68
Harris Co Toll Rd Tx 92	6.500	08-15-17	97½	6.70
Hawaii Airport Rev 91	6.750	07-01-21	98¾	6.85

Issuer
is the city, state, or government agency that borrowed the money initially.

Maturity Date
is the date when the issuer is scheduled to pay investors the full face value of the bond.

Yield to Maturity
This is the return an investor would earn by buying this bond at the quoted price and holding it until it matures in 2022.

Coupon Rate
is the rate of interest paid by the issuer. The owner of this bond will receive $63.75 per year for each $1000 of face value of bonds owned.

Current Market Value
is the last price at which the bond was traded for the day. This bond is valued at $965.00 for each $1000 of face value.

their portfolios—the interest and principal are both guaranteed to be paid by the insurer should the issuer default. This insurance earns them AAA ratings for quality. To "play it safe," should you limit yourself to only insured bond funds?

That's up to you, but let me explain a few of the drawbacks. First, remember that the guarantee is only as strong as the insurance company behind it. When Mutual Benefit Life experienced financial difficulties in 1991, it temporarily played havoc with the value of many insured bond funds that had insurance with Mutual Benefit, because their portfolios had lost their AAA status overnight. Second, because insured funds tend to hold higher-risk bonds, they are somewhat more volatile than uninsured funds (which is the opposite of what you're trying to achieve). Third, it's the portfolio manager's job to know the market and select quality holdings—why pay for that expertise and then insure the portfolio too?

If you can find an insured fund that is yielding more than a normal one, that would seem to be a good deal. But you have to ask yourself: If the insurance has value and is actually adding to the safety of the portfolio, why is the market paying me *more* to invest in it rather than less? Shouldn't higher quality go hand in hand with somewhat lower returns?

I suggest you stay with top-quality bonds rated A or better all the way.

When you call a fund that you're considering, ask them

for a breakdown of the quality-ratings of their holdings. This is often called a credit analysis, and will tell you what percent the fund has in AAA-rated bonds, AA-rated bonds, and so on. I wouldn't restrict myself to only the "insured" funds.

Mortgage-backed GNMA bond funds: much ado about nothing?

Another popular avenue to better yields are those funds that invest primarily in mortgages. Here's how it works. Let's say your neighbor Jim takes out an FHA or VA insured mortgage. The bank or S&L that made him the loan doesn't keep it on its books. Instead, it takes it and combines it with others that have terms similar to Jim's (say 30-year loans with a 10% rate). When they have at least $1 million of these loans, they sell them as a package to big institutional investors. In this way, they make a quick, small profit on the loan and have their money back to go out and make more loans.

The buyers take the package to the Government National Mortgage Association (GNMA) to be sure it meets certain standards. If it passes inspection, it is assigned a pool number to show that the timely payment of the interest and principal on every mortgage in the package is guaranteed by the "full faith and credit" of the U.S. government.

Let's assume that the Vanguard Ginnie Mae fund eventually bought the pool of which Jim's mortgage is a part. Vanguard is now entitled to have Jim's monthly mortgage payment, minus a small servicing and insurance charge, "passed through" to it from the original lender who is still receiving Jim's monthly check. And what does Vanguard do with it when they get it? They pay the interest portion out to their shareholders every month and reinvest the principal portion in more pool certificates. If you're a shareholder in the Vanguard fund, you might be the one who finally ends up with the interest on Jim's mortgage payment!

Here are some things to keep in mind about investing in a Ginnie Mae fund. The biggest drawback is that if interest rates fall, homeowners will take out new lower-cost mortgages and pay off their old high-cost mortgages. This is the "prepayment risk" that investors in these funds must carry. If that happens, then instead of receiving interest from a nice high-yield mortgage for years to come, the fund gets its money back all at once and must then reinvest it in new GNMA certificates at lower, less attractive rates. Bummer.

Also, bear in mind that the government guarantee doesn't protect you against declines in either the yield (as mortgage rates fall) or the value of your fund shares (which fluctuates daily). And your dividend checks, which vary in amount from month to month as interest rates change, are fully taxable.

The only advantage of investing in Ginnie Maes is slightly higher yields—approximately .75% to 1% per year—than are usually available with short- or medium-term bonds of high quality. If that sounds worth the prepayment uncertainty and the inherent added complexity of these securities versus normal bonds, you should investigate them further. ◆

THE FAMILY TREE OF MORTGAGE-BACKED INVESTMENTS

Fixed-Rate Mortgages

are the typical home mortgage, with a set rate for a 15 or 30 year period. Their most serious drawback is that you never know when they'll mature because homeowners have the right to prepay their mortgages whenever they can find a better deal. Funds that specialize in these have long track records for you to consider.

Adjustable-Rate Mortgages

are the kind where the interest rate is moved up or down periodically to more closely match the rates that are prevailing at that time. Funds that specialize in these are fairly new; it's too soon to see how they'll fare during a period of rising interest rates. I would suggest waiting and watching.

Collateralized Mortgage Obligations

are an attempt to eliminate some of the uncertainty caused by the prepayment risk. They do this by "putting you in line" as to when you receive principal back from mortgage prepayments rather than distributing the prepaid principal proportionately to all the shareholders at once. Don't invest in these unless you thoroughly understand what happens to the CMO's payback rate and yield if rates change by 2 or 3 points. And plan to hold them until maturity—they're not designed for easy resale.

Glossary

Average Maturity

is the average number of years it will take for *all* the bonds in the portfolio to mature. The longer the average maturity date, the greater the risk in the portfolio.

Bonds

are IOUs in the form of investment certificates.

Commercial Paper

is the name for very short-term corporate IOUs of large, creditworthy corporations. Credit-rating agencies, such as Moody's and Standard & Poor's, monitor the commercial paper market. They continually study the financial strength of the corporations which issue the IOUs, and assign ratings of 1, 2, or 3. Under SEC rules, money funds may not own any 3-rated paper because of its higher risk, and are severely limited in the amount of 2-rated paper they can hold.

Coupon Rate

is the percent of interest stated on the bond that the borrower agrees to pay to investors. It stays fixed throughout the life of the bond.

Credit Unions

are nonprofit consumer organizations, started with the idea of providing higher savings rates and lower loan rates than profit-making institutions like banks and S&Ls. Most of them are associated with trade unions or a specific company, and accounts are available only to their members; however, others have been started, especially for church groups and small communities. Many offer checking and saving services that are superior to banks and S&Ls. As for their safety, about 90% of credit unions are federally insured through the National Credit Union Share Insurance Fund. *Don't do business with one that's not.* For more on joining a credit union, call the Credit Union National Association at 1-800-356-9655, ext. 4045.

Current Yield
is the rate of return that the investor receives per year as a percent of the amount invested.

Deep Discount Bonds
are those that can be purchased far below their face value. This means investors receive, in addition to the regular interest payments, the added benefit of getting back much more at maturity than they paid for the bond originally. This extra enticement is needed either because the coupon rate being paid is below the current levels available to investors or because the issuer's credit rating has slipped and full payment at maturity is in doubt.

Face Value
is what investors are to receive when the bond matures.

FDIC Insurance

is federally-backed protection against losses in your bank account. There is a $100,000 insurance limit that applies per person (not per account). This means that all checking accounts, savings accounts, certificates of deposit, and business accounts (if run as a sole proprietorship) combined at any one bank or S&L are limited to $100,000 of protection. The $100,000 limit includes any interest you might have coming. For example, if you had $98,000 in CDs which earned $4,000 in interest before the failure, your total recovery would be limited to $100,000 and you would lose $2,000 of the interest. Not all banks and S&Ls carry FDIC insurance protection. Many rely on state-sponsored programs instead. Unfortunately, state deposit insurance has proven unreliable in many instances.

For example, in 1990 the Rhode Island state deposit insurance program collapsed. According to reports, more than 350,000 savings accounts with approximately $1.3 billion were still tied up in closed banks and credit unions seven weeks into the crisis. The rescue plan eventually paid about 60% of the depositors' money right away, another 35% in 1992 (with no interest earned in the meantime), and the rest to be paid in installments, commencing in 1998 and lasting for another 15 years! Deposits above the $100,000 insurance limit were lost. You can see the importance of dealing only with savings institutions that carry federal deposit insurance.

When it comes to FDIC coverage, there are three possible results if a bank should fail. The best is when a strong bank is found that is willing to buy the failed one. When that happens all accounts, regardless of their size, are moved to the new institution with minimal inconvenience to depositors. This is the way about 85% of the bank failures and about half of the S&L failures were handled in 1990. The second possibility is that a buyer cannot be found. Then, an "insured deposit transfer" takes place where only account balances up to the $100,000 limit are transferred to another bank/S&L. The third possibility is that the FDIC simply liquidates the failed institution and pays claims directly. With either of these last two solutions, all deposits above the $100,000 insurance limit are usually lost.

Gain/Loss
is the difference between what you paid for a security and what you got back when it was sold or it reached maturity.

Interest
is the return you get from lending-type investments, such as CDs and bonds.

Issuer
is the business or government that is borrowing the money.

Maturity Date
is the time at which the borrower is due to pay the bond in full.

Money Market Funds

are specialized mutual funds that take your money and make very short-term loans to big businesses, the U.S. Treasury, and state/local governments. They are a way of pooling your money with other small investors and getting a better deal on interest rates. Think of them as savings accounts disguised as mutual funds. They are excellent for savings or for using as a temporary holding place for money that might be needed in the near future. They are virtually as safe as FDIC-insured bank accounts but typically pay 1%-1½% more. However, there's no set level of interest that you can count on earning. You receive whatever the short-term rate is, and it changes constantly.

Governed by the Securities and Exchange Commission (SEC), the average maturity of a money fund portfolio cannot exceed 90 days, so there's not much time for something to go wrong with the IOUs. The short time period also reduces the risk of rising interest rates hurting the funds' net asset value. Other restrictions mandate that no more than 5% of a fund's assets can be invested with a single corporate borrower, and no more than 5% of the portfolio can be invested in commercial paper that carries less than the best rating.

Munis

is a slang term for tax-free bonds issued by state and local municipalities.

Par

is the face value on the bond, usually $1,000. This is what investors are to receive when the bond matures.

Total Return

is the annualized return taking both the yield and the gain/loss into account.

Wire Transfers

are a very quick way to move your money between banks. Your funds travel through the Federal Reserve bank wire system (it generally takes a few hours) and, if done early enough in the day, the receiving bank will give you credit for your money the same day you send it. Check with your bank to find out how early in the day they need to receive your instructions and what they charge for this service.

Yield

is the interest or dividends you receive each year as a percentage of an amount you invested.

Sound Mind Investing

THE FINANCIAL JOURNAL FOR TODAY'S CHRISTIAN FAMILY

Dear Valued Reader:

I hope this booklet has been helpful to you. If so, I believe you'd enjoy reading through a complimentary issue of my monthly *Sound Mind Investing* financial newsletter. It's based on biblically-based values and priorities (see pages 4-5), and gives you:

Help in setting and achieving realistic, personalized goals. You'll find no claims that I can predict coming economic events or market turns. Mine is a slow-but-sure, conservative strategy that emphasizes controlling your risk according to your age, goals, and personal investing temperament.

Very specific, timely advice. I recommend specific no-load mutual funds. For each of four different risk categories, I not only tell you what *what to buy* and *how much to buy*, but just as importantly, *when to sell and buy something else*!

Monthly "economic earthquake" updates. I include an economic primer that will help you understand the implications of the unfolding economic tremors. Plus, there are data and graphs of various economic indicators that will be especially helpful in giving us fair warning if a crisis seems to be approaching.

I'd like you to have the opportunity to see these benefits for yourself. Send in the attached postage-paid card for your free issue—there's absolutely no obligation to subscribe. I hope to hear from you soon!

☐ **Yes, send my free issue!**

Austin: I'm taking you up on your offer of a complimentary sample of your monthly *Sound Mind Investing* newsletter. Please send my free issue and subscription information to me at the address below.

Name: _____

Address: _____

City: _____

State: _____ Zip: _____

Free!
A Sample Issue of
Sound Mind Investing